HAUS CURIOSITIES

Truth in Public Life

About the Contributors

Claire Foster-Gilbert is the founder director of Westminster Abbey Institute. A public philosopher and author, Foster-Gilbert has played an instrumental role in the fields of medical research ethics and environmental issues.

Stephen Lamport was the Receiver General of Westminster Abbey from 2008 to 2018, and a member of Westminster Abbey Institute steering group from its beginning in 2013. He now serves the Abbey on an honorary basis as Deputy High Bailiff.

Vernon White is a Visiting Professor at King's College, London. He was Canon Theologian of Westminster from June 2011 until October 2018 and, from 2016, also served as Sub-Dean. White was a member of the steering group for Westminster Abbey Institute from its inception.

Edited and with an Introduction by Claire Foster-Gilbert

TRUTH IN PUBLIC LIFE

Vernon White, Stephen Lamport, Claire Foster-Gilbert

First published by Haus Publishing in 2020
4 Cinnamon Row
London SW11 3TW
www.hauspublishing.com

The right of the authors to be identified as the authors
of this work has been asserted in accordance with
the Copyright, Designs and Patents Act 1988

A CIP catalogue record for this book is
available from the British Library

Print ISBN: 978-1-912208-90-6
Ebook ISBN: 978-1-912208-91-3

Typeset in Garamond by MacGuru Ltd

Printed in Czech Republic

Contents

Acknowledgements

Sincere thanks are due to the Dean and Chapter of Westminster, the Steering Group and Council of Reference of Westminster Abbey Institute, Asha Astley, Ruth Cairns, Mark Easton, Harry Hall, John Hall, Alice Horne, Aneta Horniak, Kathleen James, Igor Judge, Seán Moore, Maurice Saatchi, Barbara Schwepcke, Ursula Williams, and Sunbeam House in Hastings.

Introduction

Claire Foster-Gilbert

This book has one task only: to cherish truth in public life. This is not a luxury. It is a moral imperative. To be more precise, making every effort to discover the truth and to tell it are moral imperatives. Giving up on the task because it is hard (and it is) or because it is contestable (which it is) or because no one has ever seen absolute truth (which they haven't) is not an option, not if we want to enjoy a civilised society in which we are free to flourish.

Taking the last difficulty first, that truth in its absolute form has never been seen, the assertion raises the question: how do we know we have never seen absolute truth? For only if we have some kind of prior knowledge of what absolute truth is can we know that what we see is not it. The letter 'O' typed here is not an absolutely perfect circle; we know it is not a perfect circle because we somehow know what a perfect circle looks like. This argument is more than mere sophistication. It illustrates the fact that truth exists and is known to us. This in turn provides the solid bedrock upon which we build the honesty, trustworthiness, transparency and reliability of our public servants and the institutions through which they serve. We may not be able to see or tell the absolute truth about any situation, but we can know how close or how far away we are from it (the 'O' is closer to a perfect circle than this 'A', for example). To suggest that truth does not exist is the most powerful contemporary way to destroy civilised, free societies, because it hands over power to those who are strong enough, loud enough and charismatic enough to assert their version of truth. George Orwell, the seventieth anniversary of whose death falls in the same year as the publication of this book, warned as much in relation to totalitarian regimes. In our time, divisive populists have taken centre stage: they attract followers and, as ideologies did in Orwell's day, they offer bright visions of a better future than the miserable lives we are currently living. But the populists' version of the truth is unstable: they may declare that two plus two equal five (an assertion Orwell found more frightening than bombs)[1] but tomorrow, because the truth is what they say it is, two plus two may equal something else. We can only judge whether they are right or not if we have the freedom and will to test the truth of their claims. We cannot afford to accept assertions lazily on the simple basis that they are made by someone we like.

Assertions of truth are contestable – the second difficulty – because they are made by us, humans with partial perspective, interests to defend, and only words as our means. Like the committee of blind people that tried to describe an elephant, each person asserting the truth of the bit of the elephant they were able to touch, we cannot see the whole. Like party politicians wanting to be elected, or secretaries of state wanting larger budgets for their departments, we all have self-interest, which skews our choice of what we claim to be true. And for all of us struggling to say what we really mean, including me writing this introduction, words cannot, in the end, be more than proximate expressions of absolute truth. So humans and their means of expression are fallible. But if public servants cease to strive to see the truth as widely as they can, defend the truth as disinterestedly as they can, and articulate the truth as clearly as they can, they also surrender society's vulnerable members into the hands of the narrow-minded, self-interested and obfuscatory. Injustice abounds if the truth is not sought in the public square. Why do public enquiries matter so much if not to ensure that what really happened to the victims is known about and at the very least is not repeated on vulnerable people in the future?

So yes, telling the truth is hard, the third difficulty. Inertia can propel us towards lazy lies. But what better purpose for a human life than to seek truth, to sustain it and to tell it? It is especially commanded of public servants who should actively protect the disinterestedness of the public square in which they operate.

The essays in this book, based upon lectures delivered in Westminster Abbey in 2018, take the points I have touched upon much further, exploring and responding to the difficulties for public servants as they seek to rule and run a world in which truth is, at best, debased. In 'Truth Pursued', Vernon White, acutely aware of the elusiveness of truth, uses compelling examples from literature to explain how it is that we rarely know what really happened anywhere, at any time, to anyone. But then he makes a powerful case for continuing to seek truth. There is nothing in the difficulties of its pursuit that denies the basic meaning or existence of truth itself. The bare notion of truth still makes sense, and this, he shows, has practical relevance. First, it establishes a goal for scientific and other pursuits: whatever the relativity and limits of our current understanding of any thing, the truth of that thing is there, and is the focus and means for our understanding to become less limited. The givenness of truth, however elusive, is also a bulwark against cynicism that deliberately exploits the difficulty of finding the truth to some other, nefarious end: deliberately misleading people, for example, in order to exert political or economic influence. White also addresses the moral question of the use to which truth is put. His essay is a powerful tool in the hands of those who want to defend truth in the face of its denigration, not least because he does not caricature the arguments he wants to address. He resists this ugly characteristic of an age in which winning an argument seems to be more important than discovering the truth.

Stephen Lamport's essay, 'Truth Sustained', is written out of his long experience of public service in the foreign office, as Private Secretary to The Prince of Wales and latterly as the Receiver General of Westminster Abbey. Many years of faithful service have taught him the wisdom of the honest pursuit of fact and reality, and of never veering too far from them. This pursuit and tenacious adherence to truth is not simple and nor is it quick or easy, because truth can take time to reveal itself: 'events may only declare their true meaning as time goes on'. But the cost to a civilised society of lying cannot be overstated. Lamport mourns the ways in which social media has magnified untruth, without accusing it of causing our post-truth culture. He calls for a rekindled adherence to the Nolan Principles of public life, which themselves have shown a commendable resilience since their articulation in 1994, but

4

he also calls on the more intangible support of the faith for which Westminster Abbey stands. In Parliament Square, the great institutions of law, parliament and Whitehall contribute to what Lamport calls, exquisitely, the 'symphony of truth', to which the Abbey, on the south side of the square, contributes its harmonic search for ultimate reality and truth.

In my own essay, 'Truth Told', I explore the many temptations away from truth-telling that each aspect of public service faces: politicians in their unceasing caricature as 'scurvy',[2] to quote Shakespeare; civil servants in their shying away from telling ministers truths they don't want to hear; judges in unconscious bias; journalists in telling the story that is 'too good to check'; and, online, nearly all of us. Truth has to be actively worked for, against the default of lazy mendacity. It is like a muscle, and the essay offers advice on training the muscle. Taking a leaf from Orwell's book, striving for clarity is essential if truth is to be told. If my language is unclear then at best I am meaningless, at worst I am deliberately obfuscating in order to deceive. Good grammar provides clarity as it ensures the proper placing of one's carefully chosen words. But words are not everything. We should not underestimate the power of delivery, particularly in the public square. We are stirred by the sound of a person, by individual words or phrases that shine out, more than by well-argued paragraphs. Rhetoric is effective, so it has to be used to serve truth, not popularity. And sometimes, words have to cease because truth will only reveal itself in silence: not the silence of collusion, but the silence of listening empathy.

Truth is hard, but in public life it is to be cherished because it is of inestimable value. Truth is hard, but it must be pursued, sustained and told, and public servants need to train to the highest standard in its defence. These essays will help furnish the means.

Truth Pursued

Vernon White

On a summer's day a hot air balloon with a child passenger in its basket was tethered in a field. But in a sudden squall it lost its moorings. The pilot, outside the basket, struggled to hold the rope. Five onlookers instinctively rushed to help, grabbing hold of other ropes as the balloon began to lift and strain towards the steep edge of the hillside. They all tried to cling on. But in the end they lost hold, or let go, as it threatened to lift them too. Except one who did not let go, who was carried into the sky as the balloon rose, dangling on the end of his rope, until he could not hold on any more. He fell to his death, watched by the horrified onlookers.

That is the opening scene of Ian McEwan's novel *Enduring Love*.[3] It is a beautifully crafted and compelling narrative deliberately leaving us with dissatisfaction and questioning. What *had* actually happened? What was the real truth? As the novel progresses the would-be rescuers tell and re-tell the story in different ways. It haunts them. Was the rope torn from them or did they let go? Who let go first? Were they half heroes, or cowards? They tried counterfactuals: if one had not let go first, what would have happened? Might all of them have managed to bring the balloon down safely?

Perhaps they could never know. Why?

Not primarily because of a lack of information. Most of the basic information they needed was visible. They were there. They were eyewitnesses, even participants – and still they did not know. So why? Because, the narrator tells us, their view was skewed by themselves. No one could know or agree what happened because their sensory data was 'warped by a prism of desire and belief, which tilted our memories... in our own favour'. Objectivity was therefore impossible. The evolutionary drive had 'winnowed it out' of them, leaving only what would favour themselves 'carved in their genes like ruts in a car track'.[4] No ideal of a disinterested pursuit of objective truth, of the kind that some metaphysics and science might at least claim, could rescue them, for these ruts of self-interest were too deep.

It is a telling account of one of the key difficulties in pursuing truth, a fictional illustration of what is the case in many real stories – political and personal, historic and recent. What really happened in the 2016 referendum, in a Whitehall meeting at which a minister changed his mind, at Dunkirk in 1940, in any story we tell ourselves about our own lives? McEwan's brutal analysis is that we rarely really know, not just because of faulty memory or lack of information or lack of conceptual grasp of a situation, but also because of this 'prism of our desires and beliefs'. It is because we are hard-wired by evolution into self-interest, which skews our memory and information with our partial perspective and our own interests. This is why the EU referendum story will always be told, believed, interpreted, in different ways by different political tribes. It is why the Dunkirk story may be told in one way by the English and another way by the French, or Germans, or any of the other nations involved. Not because some facts are unknowable, like numbers of votes cast or numbers of troops evacuated, but because facts are only one ingredient in a narrative in which *reasons* for facts and *meanings* of facts will always be seen in different ways according to the different interests of tribes or individuals. It is this realisation that lies at the heart of radical post-enlightenment suspicion about all truth, all stories we tell about ourselves and the world, whether scientific, social, religious, political or personal. It is a suspicion that leads some to give up altogether on truth because they think it is simply impossible.

So this is the central issue I want to pursue in this essay. Not how we speak truth to power (a question especially for civil servants); nor how we speak truth in power (a question especially for politicians); nor whether truth should sometimes be withheld (a question for journalists). Those are pressing and vital questions, but they will be dealt with in subsequent essays. Here I simply want to deal with the underlying question of whether we can still have confidence in truth at all, whether there is even any point and possibility in pursuing it. This is worth considering, I believe, because there is a real scepticism around about the very notion of truth, especially in public life. And this can and does lead people to give up altogether. The scepticism is driven partly by a proper recognition that truth is genuinely problematic. But also, for some, by cynically exploiting that genuine problematic for other purposes altogether.

My argument will go like this. First, we do need fully to admit to and explore the genuine problematic of truth (not least because that is part of being truthful about truth). In other words, I think we need some sympathy with Pontius Pilate's celebrated question at the trial of Jesus: 'What is truth?' That he received no immediate answer implies not just Pilate's bafflement about the particular issue of Jesus's innocence but a genuine difficulty about all truth. But then I want to argue that nothing in these genuine difficulties about truth denies the basic meaning and 'existence' of truth itself, and that is why there is always some point and purpose in pursuing even an elusive truth. What I hope the discussion will do is expose this dynamic that seduced Pilate and now seems to be beguiling us in late modernity; namely, the temptation to concede too much to the genuine difficulties of truth and so give up too soon on the pursuit. I want to expose it as a seduction that only works by an unholy alliance between the honest recognition of genuine problems and, at best, sloppy thinking about them or, at worst, a more sinister and cynical appropriation of them.

The Problematic of Truth

First then, just what is the genuine problematic of truth which we have to acknowledge in order to be truthful? Truth, whether moral, factual or historical, can indeed be problematic, elusive, complex; it is only rarely 'pure and simple'.[5] So what are the different dimensions of this complexity?

To begin with (although not the primary issue in McEwan's story) there is often a simple lack of factual information in life. This may seem improbable given the information overload now provided by the internet. But in fact we are still very limited in what we know. For all the smart speculations of the internet's algorithms, we still have only very limited and only indirect information about other people's minds and motives. Especially in the past, so this particularly limits our historical knowledge. We are also limited in access to information about natural processes. Even with computer modelling we do not get anything like direct observation of *all* that is and happens (only 5 per cent of natural reality is really known, according to current scientific estimates).[6] That clearly compromises and limits our scientific knowledge, which can also only ever be partial and provisional. There is also the problem of our limited understanding, not just limited information. Even given all relevant factual information, our actual grasp of it is always limited by our finite understanding, those intrinsic limits to our reason that Kant and others have insisted on in their critiques of human reason.[7]

Then there is this even more telling part of the problematic that McEwan's story illustrates; that is, not just our limits of information and understanding but also those inevitable distortions of information and understanding as they are shaped, selected and skewed by our perspectives and the perspectives of others, by our prior beliefs and desires, and those of others. This skewing of truth operates consciously and unconsciously, often subtly, affecting people of goodwill, not only those setting out to deceive. It affects history, politics and science, as well as routine daily life.

Underlying all this there is also the problem of communicating truth truthfully. To be sure, some factual truths (*pace* Oscar Wilde) *are* 'pure and simple' and can be accurately communicated easily (for example, the mere fact that you are sitting reading this text now *is* simple enough and easily expressed). But such simple isolated facts are not all that we need to communicate. We also need to communicate issues involving meaning and purpose (for example, whether you are reading this because you genuinely have a concern for truth in public life, or just to avoid another task, or both). To communicate that truthfully will require more than factual accuracy about your physical location and activity now – it requires a more complex and contestable wider narrative. To take a less trivial example: if a permanent secretary wants to communicate to a minister the options and implications of implementing controversial policies, whether constructing a high speed rail link, changing the stop and search policy, or going to war, it is obviously not a matter just of offering isolated accurate facts. They will have to convey options in narratives that include wider purposes and values, political realities, all embedded in other related chains of events. To communicate all that truthfully and with integrity, so that it is also *heard* truly, is as much a narrative art as an assembly of accurate factual information. Put another way, to communicate anything of real interest truthfully and effectively we all have to be poets; our words have to convey not just true factual information but they must resonate and sing in a way that conveys true meaning, which can be heard as such.[8] In poet Emily Dickinson's celebrated lines, to tell 'all the truth' we sometimes have to 'tell it slant'.[9]

In summary, the inevitability of limited information, limited understanding, distorted perspectives and complex issues of communication are all part of the genuine problematic of truth, which we must acknowledge in order to be truthful. Our best legal, scientific, historical, social and journalistic practices have always acknowledged this. That is why they always strive for more facts, better understanding, better communication, and why they employ strategies (practical and personal) to try to offset the skewing of personal bias or tribal interests. The question now is, can they ever really succeed? Is it really possible?

The Possibility of Truth

In moving from this problematic of truth to its possibility, the argument I want to make is simply that it is always possible at least to make sense of the *pursuit* of truth. It is a pursuit that has meaning, I suggest, because nothing in this genuine problematic denies in principle that there is a truth to be found, however elusive. The bare notion of truth still makes sense although it cannot always be fully grasped. This is the first crucial way of defending the pursuit – simply by maintaining the bare notion of objective truth. What I mean by this is the notion that some realities in life are just given. Whether given by God or nature or chance, some things just are the case (that is, 'true') – whether or not we agree it, know it, or like it. Not all reality is self-created, self-chosen, malleable according to our own whims. It is just there.

This bare notion of truth is incontrovertible the moment we accept there are any real distinctions in reality. Whether we are dealing in law, science, history, politics, daily life, logic, mathematics or morality, we accept there are some real and absolute distinctions to be made, even if we do not always agree about particular cases. So, for example, we accept that saying two plus two equals four is different from saying it equals five, or that saying Hitler was bad is different from saying he was good. These are real distinctions, which matter. And that is what generates the notion of truth. That four is not the same as five, that good is not the same as bad, is a matter of truth, not just preference. Only in a world of complete shapeless uniformity where everything was the same as everything else would truth have no currency, no meaning at all. But ours is a world of real distinctions, so truth does have meaning. Of course we will often disagree about what is the case in particular circumstances. But that will not invalidate this notion of truth itself any more than our failure to solve complex mathematical or moral issues invalidates the notion of mathematical or moral thinking. Such absoluteness, objectivity and non-negotiability about the notion of truth itself makes it what Plato called a transcendental: a notion that has an absolute and universal meaning regardless of the extent to which it is only relatively visible or identifiable in any particular instance.

Perhaps this point is obvious but too abstract? Perhaps it is sound but seems trivial, largely irrelevant to the concrete problems of actually trying to identify and access truth? Yes, we may say, the bare notion of truth may have meaning, and truth 'exists' in every situation even if we can't always get at it; as artist Georges Braque said, 'Of course truth exists, only lies are invented!' But does that have any relevance to the problems of actually accessing it?[10]

I think it does for two reasons, both of which bear on public life not just on philosophers' mind games. The first is because of a popular kind of appeal to relativism in public discourse which all too easily, but falsely, implies there is no meaning to truth at all – which in turn easily leads to giving up the pursuit altogether.

An example of this was provided in one of the first ever Westminster Abbey Institute events.[11] It was not challenged because it came from a distinguished scientist, but it should have been. Our scientist was describing how scientific judgements, whether a diagnosis in medical science or a model of the subatomic structures of the universe, can only be provisional truths, relative to the limited knowledge currently available, always open to revision. In itself that was unexceptionable. It was simply part of the genuine problematic of truth for us all. Much the same relativity and provisionality applies to the politician making assertions about the economy or the state of the health service, or a civil servant advising on these issues. But what our scientist then said, on the basis of this sort of relativity, was that there is therefore no absolute truth at all. That simply does not follow. Of course a true medical diagnosis or a true analysis of the deep structure of things may never be fully found – but it is still the case that a diagnosis and a structure exist in reality which is true, even though inaccessible. Moreover, even if that reality is a fluid one, entailing a constantly changing diagnosis or structure, that very fluidity would still be the case; so it would be the truth about it. The pursuit of that truth would then still be a proper goal, for science or any other discipline, whatever the relativity and limits of current perceptions.

In fact I suspect that is what the scientist meant. But it is not what he said. He said, 'there is no absolute truth', not 'we can't always get at it'. And the point is that the moment this sloppy rhetoric is allowed to go unchallenged it undermines motivation to pursue truth at all. It easily becomes a cloak for laziness, an excuse for giving up even trying to reach the truth, expressing it or living it – especially if the attempt is likely to prove difficult or costly. Just as Pilate gave up. Just as many public figures give up trying to explain complexity, resorting only to bland soundbites. So this is the first reason why it matters to keep clearly asserting what may seem obvious, that there *is* truth to pursue, however elusive. It needs to be maintained as a bulwark against laziness and moral weakness.

The second is that it will also be a bulwark against a more deliberate cynicism about truth; the denial or distortion of truth for more sinister and self-interested reasons. In other words, it will be a bulwark against our current so-called post-truth culture, which deliberately subverts the pursuit of truth.

This needs a short excursus about 'post-truth' culture, which we need to understand if we are to resist it. It is a culture in which the language of truth and virtue may still be used, but only as a cover. So rather than being used to refer to some independent, transcendent, objective meaning or metric, it is used only instrumentally, as a tool of social manipulation. In particular, it is employed as a way of destabilising enemies and bolstering friends with a sense of tribal belonging and personal identity. 'Truth' is attached to any ideas or words that have this emotionally persuasive power, either to confuse outsiders or cement insiders in our own tribe.

The words, phrases and ideas that currently have this emotive and neuralgic power are obvious. For one tribe the triggers might be 'looking after our own', 'unchecked immigration', 'taking back control'; for another tribe they might be inclusiveness, tolerance, environmentalism, progressiveness. By attaching some supposed truth claim (such as a supposed truth of statistics) to these words and phrases, each tribe gains influence regardless of the actual truth of those claims. It works because we are all ready to collude. In an uncertain world we *want* to hear what will bolster our identity, give us some sense of belonging, flatter our vanity. So we want to believe any 'truth' claims that resonate with these needs. As Augustine said: *mundus vult decipi* – the world wants to be deceived. Those who would manipulate us know this. They know how any culture needs its common neuralgia, passions and language to reinforce its sense of common identity and mission. Anyone working in corporate life, politics, church or academy will recognise this. Advertisers regularly exploit it. But it is now much more widespread in public life too.

This culture is not wholly new, precisely because it is being driven by deep visceral human feelings and needs of belonging, power and tribal identity that have long been around. However, I think today it has new intensity, particularly because it can now feed off the infrastructure of global communication and virtual social media. This not only enables the post-truth culture to spread more widely and swiftly but also helps target it to us more cleverly by using the reinforcement of our social networks. Facebook, for example, is powerful not just because of its reach (currently 1.2 billion users a day compared to, say, BBC *News at Ten* with 4.5 million) but also because of its social logic; the way it can filter an opinion to users through their own trusted tribe of friends and family so they tend to accept it without independent checks about its truthfulness.

It is also possible that post-truth culture has received new impetus from radical philosophies of postmodernism, the French anti-foundationalists such as Derrida and Baudrillard who may seem to offer formal philosophical backing to this culture. Matthew d'Ancona, in his incisive book *Post Truth*, thinks they have at least a trickle-down effect, benefiting Mr Trump and others even if they have never heard of these philosophers.[12] I am not so sure. I believe it is more likely that it is the timeless power of tribalism and the need for identity in an increasingly uncertain world that has given momentum to so-called post-truth culture, not French epistemology. But whatever its causes, whether social, technological or philosophical, the point remains. There is this culture around us, one where deep instincts of tribalism are trumping even the bare notion of real objective truth. And I do not think it is going away. Its label may go out of fashion, some push-back may occur as we become more aware of fake news and we support, belatedly, a return to more responsible mainstream media that retain some integrity in their best practice. But I suspect those drivers for personal power, identity and tribal belonging will always operate below the surface, and we will always collude with them. So the issue remains. The bare notion of truth will always need defending.

The Identifiability of Truth

However, can we also now go further? A bare notion of truth, however vital, is unlikely to survive on its own, so can we also give it more substance? Can we claim that truth, even complex truth, can and must actually be identifiable as well, at least in some measure? Can we not only argue for truth in abstract and in principle, but also in practice as an identifiable property? I think we can. We can do more than affirm some bare notion, some abstract logical implicate of reality which though real never really becomes known or found (rather like the Higgs boson particle before it was spotted); we can also argue for something that *is* genuinely knowable and identifiable, even though problematic.

The encouragement to think this is possible begins with the fact that, at least in some states of affairs, truth *is* obviously identifiable. There are some factual truths that are self-evidently identifiable. As already suggested, the physical presence of you, the reader, present in whatever time and place you currently inhabit, is not in question. Likewise the existence of the chair on which you may currently be sitting, which is present objectively not just in your mind. To be sure, these sorts of factual truths may not be so interesting or useful as more complex issues that are much harder to identify. Truths about what really happened with McEwan's fictional balloon, the state of the economy, the meanings of a Shakespeare sonnet, the existence of God, or indeed the subatomic structure of your chair, are much more interesting as well as more complex. But then the moment we accept we can at least identify truth in those simpler things, the idea that truth then retreats *wholly* over the horizon in these more complex fluid realities, so we can grasp nothing at all of it, is not plausible. Why? Because this world of real distinctions is also self-evidently a fundamentally connected world in which different things are also related things at some level. We do not live in a series of wholly random, separate, atomised realities in life. No science I know of (and no Christian metaphysic either) conceives the world wholly disintegrated in that way. Quite the opposite. This in turn makes it wholly implausible that truth itself is fundamentally fragmented, relevant only to some things and not at all to others. Things are too connected for that. The 'transcendental' of truth must be, at least in principle, findable in everything. Logic demands this and nothing I can see in the genuine problems of truth refutes it.

The nature of language itself endorses this. Although our reach for poetic language demonstrates the genuine elusiveness of truth, by the same token it also demonstrates that we can grasp at least something of it because we haven't had to fall completely silent. The very fact we have evolved poetic language to communicate at least something with the 'edge' of words, rather than retreating to silence, witnesses to porousness between simpler realities and complex realities, not complete disconnectedness. Again, that in turn gives us confidence that we can know at least *something* true about those complex realities.[13]

Above all, common sense and experience also endorse this. For in practice we do sometimes make advances in knowing the truth even of complex situations and realities. Given proper enquiry, given the best practices of empirically tested scientific, historical, journalistic endeavour (and especially when suitably disciplined by a proper humility about our limits), we do as a matter of fact acquire new knowledge even in the case of complex issues. Few if any, for example, would suggest that no advances at all were made in the Jimmy Savile inquiry's report of 2013 or the Iraq inquiry's report of 2016. We can and do get to know even difficult truths, in some measure.

In short, logic, common sense and language all encourage us to think truth really can be identifiable, as well as just present in principle. That is the second reason for defending the pursuit of truth. It is another reason to keep our nerve in pursuing truth. It is another reason to resist lazy or cynical calls to give up on that pursuit.

Why Truth Matters

Finally there is also the powerful moral imperative for the pursuit of truth, as well as these grounds from logic and common sense. To reverse Kant's dictum 'ought implies can'; if we *can* we certainly *ought*, morally not just logically.

This has already been implicit. Let me now foreground it. Especially to emphasise the moral imperative specifically to pursue complex truth, not just settle minimally for obvious 'easy' factual truth, nor just for pragmatic truth which seems to work better. The vital moral imperative is precisely to keep pressing for the whole truth, those more complex truths that include wider narratives of meaning and purpose, some of which may be difficult truths for us to accept. If we only pursue the truth about bare facts, or about the pragmatic questions of life – 'what works' – we will by definition miss all the really important moral issues. We will miss the significance of the facts, who is being benefited by 'what works', and for what purpose. These are questions that can only be answered by asking about wider truths embedded in the more complex narratives. Has not history impressed this on us time and time again? It is not enough just to know the time of a train or what pragmatically makes the trains run efficiently. We have to know the wider truth about their meaning and purpose. Where were they going and for what purpose? To Eden or to Auschwitz?

This moral imperative for pursuing the whole complex truth is evident in ordinary personal relationships. It is vital for trust, which is the foundation of all real relationships. Parents know this with their children, teachers with students, partners with their lovers, public servants with their masters, diplomats with their hosts and we know it with ourselves. Ultimately the truthfulness that tries to face reality as fully and wholly as we can is always necessary for good relations.

This is not straightforward. It has to be done responsibly, sometimes gently, gradually, because it can be painful to ourselves and others if we fully unveil reality. Humankind sometimes cannot bear too much reality all at once. As a diplomat reminded us in a previous Institute seminar, ambiguity or economy with the truth may sometimes be a necessary *preface* in good relationships.[14] Nonetheless, the fuller truth must always be honoured eventually. Even Nietzsche, so sceptical about truth and aware of its potential destructiveness, agreed. Only this 'unconditional will to truth […] which originated in spite of the fact of the [apparent] disutility and dangerousness of truth […] only with this will to truth which means "I will not deceive even myself" [as well as others] do we stand on moral ground [with each other]'.[15]

Truth is also, of course, a moral imperative for social order as well as personal relationships. In particular it is the basis of justice. The willingness to pursue and face truth without fear or favour is the vital foundation for both criminal and social justice. Thank God for the rigorous, vigorous, unconditional pursuit of truth by forensic, judicial processes and by much of the responsible press. How could we have even begun to address, for example, the whole complex event of the 2017 Grenfell Tower tragedy, so mired in vested interests and neuralgic tribal reactions, without an unconditional will to find the whole, complex truth? It is necessary for reconciliation as well as justice. Tellingly, it was a truth and reconciliation commission that helped post-apartheid South Africa move forward.

More needs to be said about how this pursuit of truth is sustained responsibly in concrete situations. But that is for other essays. For now it is just the preliminary case for truth that I want to make: we can and must make the case for trying to pursue truth, however elusive. It is a case that always needs to be made, but especially now in this culture of sloppy language and cynicism, which so easily seduces us to compromise it, give up on it, which reduces us all to Pontius Pilates.

Post Script

Such is the case for truth which can be made in terms of language, logic and moral intuition. For some, of course, there is also an even more decisive ground for truth and its pursuit to be found in religious faith and in the stories of faith. And one such story provides a particularly fitting epitaph to this argument.

That brief, telling encounter of Jesus with Pilate before his death resonates with so much of this. It is apposite in the first instance because the encounter mirrors so well much of what we have already considered. Pilate's question to Jesus 'what is truth?' invites us to see the genuine problematic of truth. Pilate's act of washing his hands also invites us to see how easily we capitulate in the face of the complexity – what else is the post-modern cry 'whatever!' but our own handwashing? As the story unfolds, faith also then invites us to reject Pilate's easy capitulation and to keep believing. It helps us see beyond the problematic of the question to offer an 'answer'.

But here it begins to offer a further dimension as well. For the answer is not offered in words or propositions, logic or even straightforward moral appeal. It is offered through the narrative that follows, the extraordinary act of Christ's personal sacrifice, vindicated in resurrection. What the biographer is telling us in dramatic form is that for all the genuine problematic in perceiving and expressing truth, there is always something to be discovered, not so much in argument but in the events of a lived life. In particular, Christ's life (explicitly claimed elsewhere as '*the* way, truth, life').

This claim suggests at the very least that such a life can be a source of *examples* of moral, social and spiritual truth. And that is not hard to see. In the case of Christ there clearly are exemplary moral truths about the equal value of all humanity, regardless of social status; there are also spiritual truths about the extraordinary creative power of forgiveness and sacrificial love; all lived out in complex human situations. But the claim also suggests more. By seeing this life of Christ as '*the* way, truth and life' his exemplary truths are given an even greater status. Their source and character appear to rest in something or someone ultimate. We are being given here an assurance that their truth is not just humanly constructed but really is an objective reality, rooted in a transcendent divine mind: God, creator of all meaning. This perhaps is why truth haunts and pursues us as much as we pursue it. It helps us understand why we have the instinct that truth will not go away just by the decree of any human fashion, human president, or philosopher. If it is of God it is indeed a 'transcendental'. This is what once again captivated even Nietzsche, the implacable anti-Christian: 'even we godless anti-metaphysicians still take our fire from this flame lit by the thousand-year-old Christian faith which was also Plato's faith, that truth is God, truth is divine'.[16]

Of course we do not have to share this faith in order to share a passion for truth and a reverence for it. I am constantly humbled by the pursuit of truth of those who have no faith. But if we do have such faith, it should surely add infinite weight to the pursuit.

Truth Sustained

Stephen Lamport

Three characters in nineteenth- and twentieth-century fiction can illustrate the lesson of why truth matters. They are Augustus Melmotte, Nicholas Salmanovitch Rubashov and Winston Smith. *The Way We Live Now*[17] is one of Anthony Trollope's longest novels, and Melmotte is the villain of the story: an unlovable and unscrupulous self-made man whose enormous wealth and success (including inviting the Emperor of China to dinner in his London house and being elected MP for Westminster) is based on an unending series of untruths which leads, in the end, to the collapse of his financial empire, his disgrace and his suicide. Rubashov is the anti-hero of Arthur Koestler's *Darkness at Noon*.[18] He is a successful party apparatchik in Stalin's Russia, whose life is ended by a bullet in the back of his head because 'truth', as defined by those in power, has moved beyond Rubashov's set of beliefs to the point where what he once stood for can no longer be tolerated. And Winston Smith, the hero of Orwell's *Nineteen Eighty-Four*,[19] moves us a step further in the realm of untruth to a world in which truth has no existence beyond the definition of the day. Winston's job at the Ministry of Truth is to extinguish yesterday's truth to the ever-changing new version handed down by the Party. This is a world in which any genuine meaning of truth is utterly abolished.

These examples highlight the starting point of my essay: that in a world which seems increasingly to have lost its high regard for truth, this mark of a genuinely civilised society is under serious threat. My argument is that truth matters, that it is under attack on a variety of fronts, and that we need to be alert to the damage of a journey which might lead in just that Winston Smith direction. To the charge that these examples from fiction do not reflect the real world in which we live, I would simply warn that fiction can be a powerful symbol and reflection of the world around us. Remember Vita Sackville-West's dedication in *All Passion Spent*: 'No character in this book is entirely fictitious.'[20]

My standing is not as a philosopher, a psychologist, a sociologist or a theologian. I am not trying to shadow Kant, Nietzsche or Hegel in setting out a world view that any right-thinking person must accept. I am simply someone with a background in public life and public service for most of my career: fifteen years as a diplomat, serving overseas and at home, including as Private Secretary to two ministers; ten years in the Royal Household as Private Secretary to The Prince of Wales, where I lived very much on the frontline of public service, public duty and a commitment to the quest for a better society; and ten years in Westminster Abbey as Receiver General, where the commitment of that great church and institution to integrity and truth can, I believe, be taken utterly for granted. It is on that basis that I wish simply to set out my personal perception. I want to explain what I see as 'truth'; why it matters in terms of sustaining civilised society;

what that might mean in today's world; and where I may see some grounds for hope. Can, indeed, truth be 'sustained'?

What is Truth?

Truth has been for centuries a problem to which philosophers have never agreed a solution. The concept is elusive once you try to pigeon-hole it into a definition. Is it knowable at all? Is all truth simply relative? Is it no more than an ever-changing approximation? But elusive as the truth is, I believe we are always searching for it, consciously or unconsciously. Seeking after the truth to explain events is, after all, the basic object of historical studies. But is that possible if historical explanation is simply conditioned by one's own ideology? Why, for example, should the Whig interpretation of history be more 'truthful' than the Marxist? The Whig historian will tell you that the story of Britain is the story of its inevitable progress – interrupted by events like Cromwell's Commonwealth of the 1650s – from medieval autocracy towards ever greater liberty and enlightenment, culminating in the twentieth-century story of Britain as a liberal parliamentary democracy and a constitutional monarchy. The Marxist historian, on the other hand, sees human society as a logical product of the internal material conditions of the time. These material conditions evolve because each society contains within itself the ineluctable seeds of its own destruction. Or is the march of events the doing, as others argue, of great individuals like Frederick the Great or Napoleon, or irrepressible ideas like nationalism or liberalism? Is truth just a means of exercising power and political influence: my truth is more powerful than yours, and I have the means to impose it? Is there any such thing as the whole or the absolute truth – as, for example, in their different ways, Platonism, Christianity and Hinduism assert? What of theological truth, which collects around the person of God or the figure of Jesus Christ? Take your pick of any of these many approaches to truth. They are all important parts of the story. The debate is endless, unsettling and confusing.

But truth is not simply an abstract concept, best left to the men and women of thought rather than action. If that were the case, where would it leave most of us who have to grapple every day in our different roles with the world around us as we find it, we who have to act, at whatever level, rather than just think? Where does truth in reality take you in terms of action? In fact a very long way, since truth is, in its essence, equally an operative dynamic. It informs morally important drivers of action like integrity, honesty, scrutiny and a sense of history. There is an ineluctable link between truth and reality, between truth and the facts: 'If I do this, what happens…?' In every day of our lives we have to make sense of the world and make choices on the basis of our understanding. Choices that should be made, according to Christianity and many religions, in a way aimed at creating good rather than evil. My own understanding of truth comes from exactly this context: truth is a practical concept related to action. Philosophers would find that a simple-minded proposition, raising more questions than it answers. But to me there is a powerful relationship between what I see as truth and the honest pursuit of approaching as near as is possible to fact and reality. Hence the related importance of honesty and integrity. That is a definition that has meaning for me as an instrument of right action, and on that basis I am able to make some sense of the world around me.

The Place of Truth in Any Civilised Society

Even if we can never be sure what 'the truth' means – that is to say, whole or absolute truth – there are still many truths about our world and many facts defining the story around us that cannot be denied. For example, it is a fact that Germany invaded Belgium on 4 August 1914. It is a fact that on 11 November 1918 the Armistice was signed and the guns in Europe fell silent. It is a fact that John F. Kennedy was assassinated in Dallas on 22 November 1963. It is a fact that Winston Churchill died on 24 January 1965.

Facts matter. They are not answers. But if you ignore or deny them, you will have no hope of interpreting the meaning of events, or deciding what the right action, or actions, in response to them might be. Understanding the meaning of those facts is, of course, where the challenge begins. Germany's invasion of Belgium in 1914 was a story to Britain and its allies of unacceptable German aggression and brutalism that threatened the whole civilised future of Europe. That is, the understanding of the 'truth' of the facts according to the victors. To Germany, however, this was a necessary and defensible exercise by a nation of the need to protect the security and interests of its people in an increasingly threatening Europe. Likewise, the Armistice in 1918 was, for the victors, the final triumph of goodness and reason over four years of horror and suffering imposed by a wicked and immoral regime. To Germany it was an act of humiliation and abuse that led to the suffering of the 1920s and the triumph of Nazism in the next decade. Beware, therefore, the simple victor's view as the answer to truth. Truth has to be wisely discovered, situations analysed, reason applied. Snap decisions may not be the key to truth, and events may only declare their true meaning as time goes on. It is important to appreciate this.

So how does truth as I have defined it matter in practice? If truth is the basis of trust, and trust is the bedrock of consent on which representative government depends, then it absolutely does matter. I offer two examples where perceptions of the truth clearly matter. First, the dimension of the Brexit argument about the UK's likely economic performance after withdrawal. Both sides of the debate argued on the basis of how they saw the facts. One was optimistic, and the other pessimistic. Argument based on fact as seen by one side became 'Project Fear' for the other. The search here for the truth was elusive and the likelihood of possibilities confusing. Only the lapse of time will begin to uncover grounds of greater certainty. But for both sides of the debate, convincing others of their perception of the truth was what mattered, that is, convincing others that their truth was closer to the facts than anyone else's. This is an ageless political fact of life. It is the essence of debate and discussion.

My second example is a genuinely landmark change in nineteenth-century British history. The deeply passionate debate in the 1840s over the Corn Laws was exactly one in which both sides claimed a monopoly on the truth. On one side were the landed classes, who sought to maintain agricultural protection in order to keep prices high and to safeguard the economy; on the other the free-traders, who argued that the abolition of trade restrictions on imported goods would bring cheaper food and an end to famine. For one side repeal would ruin British farming; for the other keeping the existing laws would do the same. When Robert Peel, the Prime

Minister, changed his mind in 1845 from support to repeal, the public debate between the two sides was as vitriolic in its own terms as Brexit has been in ours.

There will always be different versions of the truth. But there is no doubt that persuading others of the truth counts, whichever side of the debate you are on, because belief in your version of the truth gives you the means – and the power – to pursue the policy that you think should flow from it. Of course, there may be no discernible answer, and the notion of what is truth in a particular context may be no more than a chimera – at least for now. The Protestant Reformation of the sixteenth century represented, whatever else, a deep and lasting fragmentation of Christian understanding of the rightful path to God. We live with the consequences half a millennium on. But that is precisely why the proper and continuing search for truth matters so much. The key question then becomes: which of the versions of that truth, given our present knowledge and understanding, approaches the facts and the reality more closely and more honestly?

Let me put this in the wider context of the world we live in. What helps to create and sustain a civilised society? What, as Augustine asks, might be the difference between a state and a gang of thieves? That is the place of truth. What is the moral imperative to work for truth? Its hallmark is the pursuit of goodness, justice and fairness. History shows that we have frequently been very bad at achieving this to any standard at all. It demonstrates equally that, in a myriad of different ways relating to time and context, these principles have inspired and driven much of what I would call good human endeavour. And they have been notably absent when these aims have been replaced by the raw pursuit of power, accompanied by envy, aggression, intolerance, inequality and evil. Look at Zimbabwe under Mugabe among many other examples around the world.

So where is truth in all this? What part does it play? The answer is simple. Truth helps to define what the civilised behaviour of a civilised society is based on. At the level of the family, for example, why were we as children brought up never to tell lies? Because an untruth is equivalent to deception, and deception is morally wrong. This is not Tom Stoppard's cynical description of truth in his play *Jumpers*, in which George, the professor of Moral Philosophy, says: 'On the whole people should tell the truth all right, and keep their promises, and so on – but on the sole grounds that if everybody went around telling lies and breaking their word as a matter of course, normal life would be impossible [...] Telling lies is not *sinful* but simply anti-social.'[21] Nor is truth as I define it to be found in Machiavelli's advice to The Prince when he argues 'a sensible leader cannot and must not keep his word if by doing so he puts himself at risk [...] If all men were good, this would be bad advice, but since they are a sad lot and won't be keeping their promises to you, you need hardly keep yours to them.'[22] Machiavelli may work in the short term for the cynical and the unscrupulous. But truth is an absolutely vital component of the long-term good of society. The Machiavelli option destroys good governance, since lying in practice demeans and cheapens the political system and can threaten the whole basis of civilised existence. We can see all too clearly when it goes wrong in the blatant distortion of the need to link ideas – and therefore behaviour – to a justifiable or honest understanding of the facts. Think of slavery, of Nazism or of apartheid. It is not good enough to argue that those who supported these systems were simply being true to their own beliefs. That is relativism in the extreme. Equally, we have to understand that cultural norms change, and with that a perception of the meaning of the facts. How else to explain the acceptance of slavery for centuries by the Christian church? But the essence of truth is that this honesty should reflect as responsible a view as possible of the facts as we know them at the time. That test may help us to understand the past, not necessarily to excuse it. Just as scientific truth, which is constantly evolving, has to be tested always against as honest an understanding as possible of fact and reality as they are known to us.

The Value of Truth in Our World Today

How, therefore, does the role of truth actually matter in our world today? What are the implications for us all of societies or cultures or practices that place no value on the pursuit or maintenance of truth? It has been implicit in what I have said that truth is about sincerity, authenticity, integrity and mutual understanding. The opposite of truth is the lie. The lie is not about making mistakes. The lie rests on the intention behind action, the intention to mislead others when they expect honest communication from us. As Kant warns us: 'By a lie a man throws away and [...] annihilates his dignity as a man.'[23] And the essence of lies is that they beget more lies in order to maintain belief in the original lie, and so to maintain the deception. Every lie limits our future. Look, for example, at the consequences for his entire later life of John Profumo's lies in 1963 to both parliament and the Prime Minister about his personal behaviour. And more importantly, because there is a vital link between truth, integrity and trust, lying destroys trust and breeds both cynicism and relativism. This has huge implications for societies and systems of government because the lies of the powerful lead us to distrust governments, and it is not a long journey from distrusting individual politicians and governments to distrusting the political systems on which their actions are based.

Two different aspects of modern political life feed this degradation of trust. The first is that, living in an age increasingly drowning in information, we often do not know what or whom to believe. In the absence of trust the vacuum is often filled by the demand for total transparency of everything a government, or its servants, think, write and discuss. Transparency becomes a substitute for honesty. But it is not a substitute for trust, since transparency can itself genuinely discourage or inhibit truthfulness. Seeking the truth is often not a straight or obvious line: it may mean trying out crazy ideas, discussing the undesirable in order to reject it, or simply making mistakes. It may require, in short, the space for 'protected irresponsibility', which is not a space permitted by today's rules of total transparency. Trust is similarly degraded by another disturbing feature of our modern politics: the demonisation of political debate. This distances us further from the means to fasten on the truth – both by distorting the words and opinions of one's opponent, and by denying the honesty of anyone who disagrees with one's own point of view. This perceived gap between behaviour and truth, honesty and integrity, is sadly part of the contemporary malaise of British politics, shown in an extreme form in the Brexit debate, and is a gap that is not going to end soon.

It is important to understand the underlying nature of what is happening in front of us. In political discourse, the gap between the real and the imaginary is disappearing. The consensus that the truth matters in political debate, and that telling the truth remains a priority, is simply collapsing. Prudent conduct for the voter or the politician begins to seem more a matter of choosing sides than evaluating evidence. Consider again the public debate on the EU referendum. The claim that the £350 million Britain would save each week from its contribution to the EU could be added to the funding of the NHS, a claim only to be twisted or denied after the result, was one huge example of the disappearing truth of political debate and of its uncaring divorce from fact. As one lady interviewed by the BBC in a Midlands shopping centre during the campaign disturbingly told us: 'I don't know what the EU is all about, but I'm voting to leave.'

That sombre lesson of the campaigns leading up to the EU referendum goes hand in hand with the attitude that has come to be known in shorthand as 'post truth'. This has been defined in the *Oxford English Dictionary* as 'Circumstances in which objective facts are less influential in shaping public opinion than appeals to emotion and personal belief.' This is the modern way of realising Nietzsche's destructive late nineteenth-century view that 'there are no facts, only interpretations.'[24] Or as one contemporary Russian political scientist has put it: 'Truth is a matter of belief [...] There is no such thing as facts.'[25] The danger is that in this political culture, the more that false information is purveyed by those with authority as 'the facts', the more exposed society becomes to a story that need bear little relation to any objective fact at all, and the closer we edge towards the world of George Orwell's Winston Smith. As Winston's interrogator puts it: 'Reality exists in the human mind and nowhere else. Whatever the Party holds to be truth *is* truth.'[26] We are increasingly looking at a world that manipulates facts to create its own truth. Truth becomes a matter of my personal opinion today. That opinion may be different tomorrow. If it is, I may be tempted to ignore, or even deny, the view I gave you yesterday. This, in essence, is the world of the 'alternative facts' of the Trump administration, the instant soundbite tweets of the President, un-thought-through and unrelated to the reality around him, as though truth can be reduced to 280 characters and is not a product of care, reason and effort; as though complexity can be denied and only the shortcut provides real understanding.

President Trump's tweets reflect the second, longer term threat to the cherishing of truth and the maintenance of trust in our daily lives. They highlight an important aspect of the impact of social media on truth. The threat goes beyond a concern about the quality of contemporary political debate or about the distortion of truth by those in authority. This elemental neglect of truth is deeper. It stems from the most profound change in the nature of our communications over the last two decades. The essence of much social media, in the form it now exists, is that attitudes and personal feelings seem often to be more important than facts. This brings us quickly, if we are not careful, to the danger of emotion tri-umphing over truth and to the exalting of the importance of my view, whoever I am, simply because it *is* mine. It also neuters the allied virtues we need to find our way towards the truth – the virtues of discernment, scrutiny and wisdom. The power of the social media approach is reinforced by the increasing tendency to accept as 'true' only that information which fits our own opinions, instead of making the effort to base our opinions on the evidence out there. And this trend lies alongside an increasing phenomenon where anyone with access to a social media platform can claim to be a source of news. The worry about this journey is that unless we are vigilant it becomes ever harder to distinguish fact from fiction. Everyone, and no one, becomes an 'expert' – even though we are now told by some politicians that the day of the 'expert' is over since they are unnecessary and untrustworthy. Another victim of the assault on truth.

The gap between fact and opinion, between the real and the imaginary, and between emotion and truth, is widening before our eyes. The impact of this is that much greater because of the extraordinarily powerful marriage today between culture and technology. Data on the web is immediately available to everyone, instantly, across the globe. This data is often raw and unfiltered, and probably too often unchecked and unanalysed. The result of the instant communication which lies at the heart of social media is that 'A lie can travel halfway round the world while the truth is still putting its boots on.'[27] A study found that fake stories spread on social media significantly further, faster and deeper than true stories.[28] At its worst, therefore, there has never been a faster way to propagate a lie than to post it online. This approach is most nefarious when it is deliberate, like the activities of Russian hacking, for which convincing evidence grows, to influence the US presidential election in 2016. It may be entirely innocent, for example simply reporting a story that happens to fit with our own preconceptions. But the result can be equally powerful and destructive, and each approach benefits from a culture that may be unwilling, or unable, to check the facts or exercise responsible judgement. Data and truth – information and wisdom – are not the same thing.

There are, of course, counter-arguments. There is a growing view that we are beginning to see a return to the more developed and thoughtful writing of the traditional media. I certainly hope so. I know that a commitment to the pursuit of truth in its reporting and analysis is deeply embedded in the BBC. That is a continuing source of hope. There is a view that parts of our digital world are helping to establish a greater truth for us. Wikipedia is described as a powerful example of a myriad source of facts which is helping to establish and balance those facts in a self-regulatory way that brings an ever-increasing closeness to truth. Wikipedia may indeed be a bulwark of truth in a digital age. But alongside the importance of this *Encyclopaedia Britannica* of the web lies the wider anarchy of unsubstantiated opinion all around us, which is easily and pervasively presented as fact; and the equal risk of an unspoken assumption that today's view is the right view, and thus an unspoken denial of the importance of inherited knowledge, contained not least in our books, which one generation bequeaths to the next. These contemporary trends increase the challenge to truth. The further our use of artificial intelligence comes to dominate our methods of communicating the way in which we relate to the world around us, the way in which we think, reflect and act, the more worrying the longer term implications become, and the more we need to recognise the implications of where we are. That recognition is vital. As Simon Schama said in a broadcast about the cruel destruction of Palmyra in Syria: 'We recognise what civilisation is by the shock of its imminent loss.'[29]

My argument is that the sustaining of truth is under threat, and that the maintaining of truth in our political society and our culture matters mightily. But this is not – at least not yet – a doctrine of unadulterated gloom and despair. So where do I look more widely for hope and reassurance? Where might we search for the values that should inspire the civilised society that I maintain is a fundamentally precious part of our shared lives, and for those constant and unchanging values we have recognised over centuries and have tried, however imperfectly, to realise?

My Grounds for Hope

Let me describe two sources of comfort, one about public service – whose moral underpinning Westminster Abbey Institute exists to foster – and one about belief.

In 1995 the Committee on Standards in Public Life, established the previous year by John Major, published as its first report 'The Seven Principles of Public Life' – the Nolan Principles – which set out a code of good practice for all government departments.[30] These seven principles may be self-evident to some, but they are important for us all as a guide to excellence in public service generally. They have survived the test of time and bear repeating: they are selflessness, integrity, objectivity, accountability, openness, honesty and leadership. These principles are in their essence a reaffirmation of the central place in public service of truth as I have defined it. They reflect a striving after truth. Truth inhabits them all. Without a powerful sense of truth lying at the heart of them they would have no meaning or impact. That identity with truth as a goal matters. As theologian Janet Soskice put it in a lecture for the Institute, 'Truth is both a given and work in progress.'[31] If the Nolan Principles do define the framework within which public service is expected to work, we have not lost our understanding of why truth matters in the ordering of our society, and where good may be found.

But these principles are not a magic key. The task of public service in striving to do the right thing is hard and complicated. If a fundamental part of the civil servant's role is to work for the good of society, given the multitude of conflicting pressures and constraints which they must work under every day, doing what is right is impossible without a moral road map. That map is the Nolan Principles. Those principles are defined by a striving after truth. But whose truth? One government's 'truth' is not another's. Governments set the boundaries of where they want the 'truth' to be, and that will direct and may distort the role of the civil servant to 'tell truth unto power' since, as we have seen, a government is capable of defining the truth only in terms of what it wants to believe. Once a government is set upon a particular course of action, the civil servant's task will then be only to deliver the best answer – best in relation to that defined path of truth – that they can achieve in the circumstances. Think of the decision to go to war with Iraq in 2003. Think of the Brexit negotiations where, whatever side of the debate you are on, a civil servant's task is to make the best of the excessively challenging hand they have been dealt.

And there are occasions when the action needed relates only to a part of the truth, not to the truth of the entire issue, or where the issue is such that different aspects of the truth have different weight. There is one such example in my own painful experience of an episode in 1989. Britain's relations with Iraq became embroiled in the fate of Farzad Bazoft, a dual national British-Iranian journalist who was arrested by the Iraqis, accused of spying, and sentenced to death. One hard-nosed view would have been: to preserve the quality of our wider, but difficult, relations with Iraq, to protect our trade and the jobs in Britain that stemmed from it, we should let Iraqi justice take its course. But that dimension of the truth carried less weight against a more urgent and important truth: the threat to the life of a man given no recognisably fair trial who, whatever the wider politics, should not be allowed to die in that way. My colleagues and I used every diplomatic weapon we could over a hectic and desperate weekend, including personal intervention by the Prime Minister, to persuade the Iraqis to be lenient. We failed, and the man was executed. My point is that reality and truth are often multilayered. The choices they provide may be contradictory and uncomfortable. Without a moral map to guide an understanding of where truth should lead you, making those choices will be arbitrary, or simply wrong.

The Nolan Principles help to provide this moral map. And Westminster Abbey Institute sees this commitment to the pursuit of truth vividly in its many contacts with public servants of all kinds. That is not to view public service in a misty-eyed or over-forgiving way. There are faults, blemishes and inadequacies wherever we care to look. But if those committed to public service are guided by these aspirations, as I believe they overwhelmingly are, however impeded in delivery they may be by resources, inconsistent leadership, public misunderstanding or misrepresentation by the media, this is a beacon of light in the core of our system of governance, a cause for hope.

Alongside these principles of good governance is the more pervasive, yet more intangible, support of religious belief itself. Westminster Abbey is one of the great glories of English Gothic architecture. The Abbey is a majestic canvas on which is painted the outpourings of centuries of human creativity and commitment. Its stones and spaces have echoed every single day for a thousand years to prayer and the recognition of our imperfections as human beings. The Abbey is a powerful, reassuring and lasting symbol of our commitment to the importance of truth and of the importance of striving after that truth. Other important symbols in the very nature of Parliament Square lie around it. Law, parliament and Whitehall are all contributors in their different ways to the symphony of truth in our society, as is the Abbey in its enduring search for ultimate reality and truth. For each of these institutions this pursuit should be a fundamental responsibility. In the pursuit of scientific truth, there is always more to achieve and to understand if we are to make the right choices for a civilised society. But unlike the pursuit of scientific truth, we constantly find ourselves inventing and reinventing ideas and strategies that ignore or misunderstand the facts around us. Our history is littered with examples of such abject failures. Yet in the Abbey's majestic embodiment of Christian faith, alongside all that Christian belief represents, there is a fundamental affirmation of why truth matters, why the continuing struggle to recognise where truth lies can never be ignored, and why that struggle must not cease.

Sustaining truth is a commitment, a struggle and a process. It will always be easier to recognise where we have made past mistakes than to ensure the right choices for the future. But if we are to make progress in building a fair, just and genuinely civilised world, if we are to work insofar as we ever can for the triumph of good over evil, we cannot afford to withdraw from the conscious struggle to frame our actions according to an honest perception of where truth lies. While we pursue that course, we must be alert to whatever threatens that ideal. Truth unsustained is a society ultimately compromised. The choice before us, as individuals and as members of society, is ultimately whether we seek to sustain that truth, or to undermine it.

Truth Told

Claire Foster-Gilbert

Following in the illustrious footsteps of the previous two essay-ists, I offer a literary allusion to support the thesis of my essay on telling the truth. Vernon White and Stephen Lamport gave you Ian McEwan, Anthony Trollope, Arthur Koestler and George Orwell. In turn, I give you a woman writer of great note, Richmal Crompton, whose famous protagonist, known the world over as Just William, struggles with truth.

Indulge my recounting of the story 'William's Truthful Christmas'. On the Sunday before Christmas, the vicar deliv-ers a stern warning. Untruthfulness 'poisons our social life', he declares. He challenges his congregation to 'cast aside all deceit and hypocrisy', at least during Christmas itself.

For once not tormenting the curate by staring at him unblinkingly, or accidentally letting his stag beetle escape from its matchbox and make its way up his sister's arm to her neck, William hears what the vicar says, and the words make a deep impression on him. He decides to 'cast aside all deceit and hypocrisy', and speak the truth, at least on Christmas Day itself.

Christmas Day dawns. After the presents have been opened, William's aunt thanks him for the pin cushion he has given her. True to his resolution, William explains carefully that it was 'left over from Mother's stall at the Sale of Work, and Mother said it was no use keeping it for next year because it had got so faded'. William is equally careful to explain to his uncle that *his* present, a leather purse, is a birthday gift discarded by his father because the catch doesn't work. When Lady Atkinson arrives ('One of *the* Atkinson's, you know,' whispers Aunt Emma) she gives as her present to the family a signed photograph of herself. There are 'murmurs of surprise and admiration and gratitude' from the adults, but William, when asked what he thinks of it, replies that the photographic image is 'not as fat as you are'. His parents protest at his impoliteness.

> 'Impolite?' said William, with some indignation. 'I'm not trying to be polite! I'm being truthful. I can't be everything. Seems to me I'm the only person in the world who is truthful and no one seems to be grateful to me. It *isn't* as fat as what she is,' he went on doggedly, 'and it's not got as many little lines on its face as what she has and it's different looking altogether. It looks pretty and she doesn't ...' [32]

Lady Atkinson storms out and the fury of the family turns upon William, inexplicably to him, while his uncle, equally inexplicably, slips him half a crown.

My essay is in two parts: first I will explore how thankless and difficult a task telling the truth in public life can be, and how often circumstances prevail against it being told. Second, I will suggest that our truth telling is like a muscle that needs to be exercised or it atrophies, and offer, with the confident hypocrisy of one who frequently fails to make it to the moral gym, some exercises to help keep the truth-telling muscle supple and in good shape.

The Difficulty of Telling Truth in Power

Let us begin with politics: speaking truth *in* power. Politicians start with a very great disability in this regard, for they have always been thought of as liars. All the way back in the sixteenth century Shakespeare had a multitude of insults for politicians, such as Lear's advice to the blinded Gloucester to 'get thee glass eyes, and like a scurvy politician seem to see the things thou dost not.'[33] We probably laugh with, rather than challenge, the oft-quoted quip (wrongly) attributed to Mark Twain that 'Politicians are like diapers, they need to be changed often, and for the same reasons.' It is notable how often even people who are genuinely politically engaged and supportive of democracy make strong generalisations such as 'they're all in it for themselves' and 'you can never trust a politician', or simply laugh out loud when I tell them I run an institute for ethics in public life.

Ipsos MORI bears out my experience: in 2019 its 'veracity index' had politicians at the bottom of every list of professionals whom we do, or rather don't, trust: lower than estate agents, journalists and advertising executives. (The top five *most* trusted professionals are nurses, doctors, dentists, teachers, engineers and professors.)[34]

A verbal habit of President Trump has strengthened the perception that politics, by its very nature, cannot be truthful. 'It's political' is a phrase he often uses to describe accusations made against him, defending himself and in the same breath attacking his accusers for their insincerity. If 'it' is political 'it' cannot, by definition, be true. So 'political' has become a synonym for 'untrue', and public service is divorced, on the instant, from truth.

In the face of such a sustained assumption about a politician's trustworthiness, how easy is it to adhere to the truth? How would any of us feel if we were consistently not believed, no matter what we said? How soon would we give up and simply, for ease, say the things that serve to ensure our re-election? In other words, revert to a default setting of weak people pleaser?

The pressure not to tell the truth is increased by further challenges, related to our other attitude to politicians alongside our mistrust, and that is our childish wish that they would make everything all right. Another Ipsos MORI poll, commissioned by King's College London, reported 60 per cent of us believing that we expect more of our government than we do of God.[35] So, on the one hand we have no faith in our politicians, and on the other we want them to be more powerful than the Almighty. This glorious inconsistency of the human heart is resonant with the way we view our parents. Our childhood lasts as long as they seem all-powerful to us; and ends on the day we learn they have feet of clay. Most young people then have to go through a desperately painful period of adolescent hatred and rejection as they readjust to a world in which they cannot simply leave it to their parents to make it all right, and commence the long journey into adult responsibility. But with the electorate and our politicians it seems that instead of passing through the rejection period and into responsible adulthood, we are stuck in a cycle where, at election time, we return again and again to our infant state of wanting them to make it all right for us and, having voted them in, hating them when they don't. There was a phenomenon called 'Cleggmania' in 2010 in the United Kingdom, which swiftly turned to Cleggphobia once Liberal Democrat leader Nick Clegg found himself part of government and forced by circumstances to renege on previously made promises. Without a shadow of a doubt, if Labour leader Jeremy Corbyn had won the June 2017 election and become Prime Minister, he would have met with the same callous fate. The 'Corbynmania' of that year would have curdled to Corbyn loathing as he dealt, or failed to deal, with the outcome of the EU referendum, and faced compromise after compromise of his party's dreams for us all. The media did not coin the term 'Johnsonmania' in 2019, but he too will face the electorate's disillusionment as he inevitably fails to fulfil campaign slogans. For most of what a government has to deal with when *in* power comes from external forces *beyond* its power, and with the best will in the world can only struggle to implement some of its manifesto promises, while having to attend to 'events, dear boy, events'[36] as they roll towards it in relentless waves.

I suppose we all, including politicians, harbour a secret hope that someone *will* make it all right. Most people enter politics because they want to make a difference. But given the fact that no matter what you say, people will swing from calling you Messiah to calling you a scurvy fake, which politician is going to campaign on a ticket of promising to try hard not to fail too much? And, like Just William's family, who among their colleagues is going to thank them for such honesty?

The Difficulty of Telling Truth to Power

Politically independent parts of our constitution are required, by means of their neutrality, to tell truth *to* power. These are the Civil Service, the Judiciary and the uniformed and intelligence services.

The Civil Service brings into being policies determined by democratically elected ministers. The values of civil servants, then, are bureaucratic: they must make the policies work, whatever they are, *unless*, and this is critical, the policies are barmy, that is to say, not possible to implement without some form of unacceptable harm. The civil servant's word for 'barmy', incidentally, is 'brave'.

The intention is that the civil servant will have recourse to empirical evidence and objective knowledge in order to make the minister's wishes come true, or say so if they cannot be. But civil servants are not automata: they, like the rest of us, have particular perspectives and beliefs and emotional commitments, any of which could be accused of having influenced their interpretation of the facts, however determined they are to set them to one side. Civil servants might say to a minister in all conscience that a policy may not be possible, and the minister simply doesn't accept their advice. The minister might say: 'Find me someone who does believe this can be done'. Is the civil servant to step aside? Is the question one of talent, or perception, or belief, rather than truth? What is happening psychologically here? Do civil servants, on the grounds that truth will always be partial, try simply to please the minister, because after all the minister might be right? Or do civil servants stick their heels in and assert themselves? The threat to truth for the civil servant comes in the form of over-confidence or, equally, under-confidence in the force of their arguments. The 2018 Kakabadse report on the Civil Service[37] demonstrates that sometimes the pressure on civil servants to shy away from telling the truth is considerable, where not to do so, thereby infuriating their minister, would be career destroying; but if they do shy away, the ones who pay the price are the frontline staff who have to implement barmy policies, often too quickly, and face the uncomprehending fury of the public, who cannot understand how something could have been foisted upon them that is so unthought-through. Brexit has brought these pressures to bear more fiercely and uncomfortably than this generation has ever seen before. Telling the truth is indeed a thankless task for the executive, as they attempt the complex task of unpicking 47 years of relationship and regulation without doing too much damage to the country. By contrast, working to respond to the Covid-19 pandemic, though fraught, has been something of a relief, because the policy goal to save lives is unquestionably shared, if not always the means to achieve it.

The Judiciary is protected from the morally corrosive forces that attend upon having to seek election. The cost is that the people do not choose their judges, even indirectly, and so responsibility falls upon judges to ensure that their judgements are just, faithful to the facts of the case and attentive to the balance of the arguments put to them, in order to honour the power they have been given. To be true to their call to administer justice 'without fear or favour'[38] they must guard against unconscious bias. Being aware that one might be unconsciously biased is not enough: active steps have to be taken to prevent it, but asking judges to undergo such training does not always win their gratitude.

Recognising the effect of unconscious bias on perception, the police have consciously shifted towards a policy of believing victims who come to them, particularly in the case of victims of sexual and domestic crimes. Clarity and truth are hard to establish in the fraught hinterland of domestic violence, where women (usually) and children have not only not been believed by others but also not trusted themselves, harbouring devastating and confounding notions of responsibility for their abuse. But simply assuming the victim *has* been abused has other consequences, most of all for the fairness of the trials of the accused perpetrators, who are thereby not assumed innocent until proven guilty. The case of Carl Beech in 2019 demonstrated this danger.

Frontline police have to act swiftly in circumstances that are tortuously complex. In any one scene to which an officer might be called, social and economic deprivation, histories of abuse, mental health difficulties, gang pressure, drug or alcohol addiction and racial or religious hatred could all be among the presenting issues. They would keep a moral philosopher in food for thought for a decade. Frontline police officers do not have that luxury; they must decide in the moment what is the right course of action, with sufficient assurance to win the confidence of the public – who can complicate matters further by their presence at the scene.

The armed forces and intelligence services usually, though not always, operate within a more controlled theatre of conflict or espionage, and do not usually have the pressure of a messy public or media presence. Like civil servants, their tasks are set by their political masters, but they enjoy operational independence. On the frontline there is no scrutinising body; so how do the forces ensure they see the circumstances clearly, respond with integrity, and report back faithfully so that future policy decisions on security matters are educated by true experience? How do spies retain their integrity when they are under pressure to gather and analyse information, and no one is watching them? There is more transparency in the intelligence community than before,[39] and the armed forces do now have a scrutinising presence in the theatre of war, known as 'embeds' – journalists who accompany them on their tours of duty and, embedded with them, see all that the soldiers see, but transparency is not the same as truth.

The Difficulty of Telling Truth about Power

Journalists are public servants too, though they are not always thought of as such. Their role is to tell the truth *about* those in power. Journalists are free to speak in this country, and the freedom that they have is, precisely, the freedom to speak the truth. Lying is for a censored press. The value of a free press cannot be overstated: it is an absolutely essential characteristic of a civilised society. By means of our free press, government, business and the activities of foreign powers can be called to account without fear of reprisal. We may loathe the crude headlines and bemoan the lack of accuracy, but suppose our press was prevented by our government from creating them? Imagine reading a news story that you knew had been censored or even generated by the government? How soon would you start to mistrust the government? The odd irony is that our trust, such as it is, arises precisely because the government allows itself to be criticised, often unfairly, in the press. And yet our assumption can be that we mistrust the government *because* of the media's reporting.

So for a journalist, the crime of telling a story that is 'too good to check' far, far outweighs the damage that might be done to reputations by reporting truthfully. And that is the challenge to the journalist: not to be beguiled into weaving a better narrative than the one that is tied to the facts; because we all love a good story. Contrary to appearances, social media does *not* make journalists of us all. We do not all have the journalist's skill of seeking out the truth and telling the story clearly and well; nor do we have the inclination: we are *rubbish* at telling each other the truth online. As ill-educated opinions flood the ether and untrue stories travel 70 per cent more quickly than true ones (retweeted by humans, not by bots), as a 2018 research project for MIT found,[40] journalists – real ones – are needed more than ever. In the world of journalism, fake news is a logical impossibility. If it's fake, it isn't journalism.

The Difficulty of Telling the Truth in Science and the Arts

Science and the arts are two areas of life which can and should be drivers for truth. They are forms of public service at the deepest level, finding and setting cultural norms, generating ways of seeing the world that we all, knowingly or unknowingly, adopt.

In the world of science, there are two strong biases that tempt the scientist away from telling the truth. The first, recognised by philosopher Karl Popper (and by good civil servants), is that once you have generated a hypothesis, it is nearly impossible *not* to see it demonstrated in the data around you.[41] Popper urges scientists, once they have articulated their hypotheses, to construct experiments that seek consciously to *disprove* them. In his autobiography, Charles Darwin describes the great dismay of his companion on a geological field trip when Darwin found a tropical fossil that appeared to disprove all that geology knew 'about the superficial deposits of the midlands counties'.[42] Safe assumptions were being overturned, and arguably it took a great scientist like Darwin, open to new explanations, to see what was actually there. His companion would not have found that fossil, I contend. He simply would not have seen it because he wasn't looking for anything beyond what he believed to be true. Other than her true fans, haven't we all (including me) assumed that the author of the *Just William* books is a man called Richard, not a woman called Richmal? We have seen how these pressures and tendencies have made themselves felt in the attempts to establish reliable evidence upon which to base policy-responses to the Covid-19 pandemic.

The second pressure against the truth is from what we might call 'the burden of the anomalous experiment'. Nobel Laureate Sir Paul Nurse tells a story of the experiments he ran to test a hypothesis he had formulated in his early days as a research scientist. He ran his experiments over and over again, and the results consistently neither proved nor disproved his hypothesis, but demonstrated an anomaly he could not explain. Nurse had a young family and a mortgage. By the system of ranking of universities and the way in which professional academic careers are judged, scientists, like all academics, are under enormous pressure to publish. Nurse sat contemplating the failure of his experiments, with, as he describes it, an angel on one shoulder and a devil on the other. The devil reminded him that only he had seen these results, that he could fudge them and publish in a second-rate journal, that he would never be offered a job without a publication, that without a job his mortgager would foreclose and his babies would starve. Above all, no one but he, Nurse, knew the truth of his experiments. The angel, sitting on his other shoulder, told him that he was a scientist, that his duty was to tell the truth about the experiments that had failed, even though it meant he would not be published, he would not be offered a job, his mortgager would foreclose and his babies would starve.

Nurse found a third way, the most truthful way of all, which was to accept the anomaly the experiments showed. That choice led him to further research, culminating in his Nobel prize for his contribution to cancer treatment, so the story ended well for him and for humanity. But he wasn't to know that as a young and burdened scientist on his own in the laboratory with no one to check up on him and only his own conscience to attend to.[43]

We deeply rely upon our scientists to honour the truth, to run properly designed experiments and to be open to new possibilities. But where do hypotheses come from? Made famous by Archimedes' cry of 'Eureka!' ('I have found it!'), scientists' 'eureka' moments come when they see what has not been seen before. And here they are helped by artists. For the arts, telling the truth must involve being open to that which is beyond calculation or ordinary rationality. The artist above all should reach to articulate what has not yet been seen, to point to hitherto unimagined possibilities, and hence to be the most open of us all to the chaotic and unknown. Like mystics, artists must empty themselves of all that stands in the way of simply seeing. That is their gift. Their temptation is to take refuge in the known, particularly if it has already made them famous.

Truth as a Muscle Needing Exercise

Truth is not easy. It is something we have to actively work towards in our different fields, not something that we can ever take for granted. It requires an effortful discernment and courageous intention against forces of complacency and inertia. It is like a muscle that, without exercise, atrophies, but using it can be risky, lonely and often apparently inadvisable on utilitarian grounds. Like Just William's family, most of us cannot bear too much reality.

I am as culpable as the next person with regard to telling the truth; I often lie, wittingly or unwittingly, and I am as prone as any to go with the flow of 'groupthink', as the Chilcot report called it.[44] So I write in the spirit of one fallible soul to another, offering some thoughts on how to cultivate truth telling; on what exercises, as it were, our sessions at the moral gym might include.

First, in policymaking, I wish we could all – government and people alike – learn from scientists and cultivate a research mentality. During the twentieth century, medicine became methodical in its approach to research, recognising that a good bedside manner is not enough to be a good doctor, and experience can lead to bias as well as wisdom. Pharmaceuticals need licences to be awarded only when they have been proven to work. Treatments are now developed over an extended period of time. First they are presented as a theoretical possibility, then molecules are tested in the laboratory, then turned into recognisable medicines but tested on a few healthy human beings, then on those who have the condition the treatment is intended for. A licence to market a drug is not granted until enough research has been done to justify such a decisive step. What if policies were to be developed with that same spirit of discovery, rather than with the pressure of having to find solutions straight away to problems we may have inadequately identified in the first place? It's a tall order, and there are many reasons why it would be difficult, but the mentality that allows government to learn, and society to evolve, from trial and error is a desirable alternative to a government of false promises and an infantilised electorate. And what else is the digital revolution for, if not to facilitate such an approach? Importantly, there is an existing, robust ethical framework from medical research to learn from. This interrogates the moral desirability of, first, the aims of the research and the rigour of its design; second, what is to be done to patients in order to carry out the research; and third, whether patients consent to participate.[45] How much harder, of course, for a minister to have to wait until what would be the equivalent of the licensing moment before announcing a new policy; but how great the prize when the announcement will be actually true, rather than a hopeful promise. Our moral exercise here, then, is to cultivate a mindset that is always open to new learning and to the hitherto unknown or unthought-of.

The research mindset is of necessity a humble one. Humility

in acknowledging one's fallibility is my next suggested 'exercise'. It is a critical but counter-cultural skill for people in public office. In Westminster Abbey Institute's Fellows' Programme we include a session on 'facing fallibility', in which we give ourselves permission and the opportunity to connect at a deep level with the things inside us that make us ashamed or fearful. We use an imaginative technique in which we feel our way to our places of what the Christian saint Ignatius of Loyola called 'desolation', or vulnerability. The practice is like coming to meet a dear friend who is in tremendous pain, and sitting down with them. You can do nothing to relieve the pain, but you are not going to desert your friend. The experience is surprisingly energising and joyful, as well as honest. We discover that our weakness is where our strength is to be found, but the weakness has to be acknowledged and not suppressed. This discernment process is the opposite of achievement and superiority, and it is creative: we discover that 'our deepest fears are the dragons guarding our greatest treasures', as the poet Rainer Maria Rilke put it.

Acknowledging our fallibility means acknowledging we need help. This in turn obliges us to seek good company: those who believe that telling the truth is important and will hold us to it, people whom we love and respect and whom we would let down if we failed to try to adhere to truthfulness. Then we have to ensure we are in the company of those who challenge our suppositions. It is no good, if you are in public office, surrounding yourself with those who agree with you. The story of John F. Kennedy taking on his own devil's advocate who was to be present at all his meetings and deliberately disagree with him is a fine one, whether it is true or not. A contemporary manifestation of the devil's advocate is the 'Chilcot person' whose role is to challenge groupthink. An important benefit of this exercise of welcoming diverse voices is that it helps us to cultivate proper indifference, so that we are not too quickly loyal to a point of view. Those who cultivate indifference see most clearly, because they are not compelled. This indifference is an active state, like keeping one's balance. It is not a default state: neutrality never is.

Listening inwardly is another exercise to try. The late, lamented Tessa Jowell took her moral and spiritual health as seriously as she did her physical health. Even when she was at the height of her seniority and had the fullest life imaginable as a cabinet minister, constituency MP and family woman, every year Tessa Jowell spent a week in a remote monastery, in silent retreat. This brought her to her own essential self, its fallibility and its strength, and gave her space to listen to, in her case, God. Anyone who has done this in good faith will know that this exercise is a million miles from the assumption behind crude questions to politicians about whether 'God' told them to do something. The discernment of movement of spirit is a tender, vulnerable thing of deep honesty, and should not be exposed too quickly to the electric light of publicity.

Tessa Jowell spent a second week each year in a place of the greatest deprivation she could find, for example the 'jungle' refugee camp in Calais, or the Dharavi slum in Mumbai. Facing the worst deprivation in the world put everything else into perspective for her and gave Jowell a proper sense of her relatively insignificant, but nevertheless important, place in the scheme of things. What might you or I do to ensure our perspective is regularly restored?

Telling the truth means, for most of us, the use of words above all. This, too, takes practice. Another children's book containing adult wisdom, Gerald Durrell's *The Talking Parcel*, includes a character called Parrot.[46] Parrot is the Keeper of the Dictionaries. His job is to keep words alive, and they only stay alive if they are used. So every year he would read out every word in the dictionaries aloud; but since one outing a year wasn't much to live on, he would use as varied and rich a vocabulary he could for all the rest of the time so the poor darlings went out as much as possible. 'Never use get, got, nice or terrible,' taught my superb and terrifying headmistress at primary school. You can be much more accurate, and therefore truthful, if you take time to find more precise verbs and adjectives than these overused words. Such care with language avoids 'anaesthetising the brain', the effect of using the dead metaphors and hackneyed phrases rightly criticised by George Orwell.[47] Grammar clarifies, because you have to be clear about what is the subject, what is the verb and what is the object of each sentence.

A paragraph is a unit of writing, as former *Sunday Times* editor Harold Evans taught,[48] not a sentence and certainly not a tweet. A paragraph should be beautifully formed around a single point, explaining, justifying and supporting it. The exception is the pithy saying or apophthegm, but these are rare indeed, the product of a fine-tuned mind. Wouldn't it be wonderful if all our tweets were of such calibre? There would only be one or two a year.

Truth is not just found in the words themselves or in the way they are framed. It is found in the cadences of speech, the poetic effect, the tone. As a barrister and teacher of advocacy told me many years ago, 'The money is *down here.*' Rhetoric matters because we are moved by the way someone delivers their words, not just, not even mainly, by the force of their arguments. So it is essential that rhetoric is brought into the service of truth, not power or popularity.

And sometimes, silence is the best form of truth of all. I emphatically do not mean the silence that amounts to collusion: indeed, *that* silence tells its own truth. It is a matter of some considerable pride that most visiting overseas heads of state see noisy demonstrators against the atrocities of their regimes on our streets; restrained, yes, but also protected and not silenced by our police, as with the visit of the Saudi Prince in 2018, when a vocal group set itself up opposite Downing Street and loudly demanded an end to the war in Yemen; and our own LGBTQ+ demonstrators outside Westminster Abbey at the time of the Commonwealth Celebration, protesting against abuse in some Commonwealth countries. Sadly, when President Trump visited, Whitehall and Parliament Square were cleared. That felt like collusion.

The silence I mean is revelatory silence, as we give ourselves the chance to rest from our busy lives and chattering minds; to stop and 'look at our hurt hands' as Pablo Neruda puts it in his poem 'Keeping Quiet';[49] to give, too, our overused, soiled and toiling earth a rest. This is the silence within which the truth might emerge.

When I delivered the lecture upon which this essay is based, I finished it with silence. I said that we are in a holy place. The walls of Westminster Abbey have heard the prayers of people like us for hundreds of years, people seeking understanding, wisdom, peace, justice, all underpinned by truth. I said that we are once again in troubled times: the burden of public office is heavy; it is easy to be despondent; we can draw strength from the listening silence of this place and the good company we are in tonight. I said, quoting Neruda's poem, that I will count to twelve, and you will keep quiet, and then we'll speak again. You might try it now.

Notes

1 George Orwell, 'Looking Back on the Spanish War' (1943), essay available at https://orwell.ru/library/essays/Spanish_War/english/esw_1 (accessed 29 January 2020). The full quotation reads: 'If the Leader says of such and such an event, "It never happened" – well, it never happened. If he says that two and two are five – well, two and two are five. This prospect frightens me much more than bombs – and after our experiences of the last few years that is not a frivolous statement.'

2 William Shakespeare, *King Lear*, ed. R. A. Foakes (London: Arden Shakespeare Editions, 2018 [1606]), Act IV, Scene 6, line 171, p. 340.

3 Ian McEwan, *Enduring Love* (London: Vintage, 1998).

4 Ibid., pp. 180–81.

5 'Jack: That, my dear Algy, is the whole truth, pure and simple. Algernon: The truth is rarely pure and never simple.' Oscar Wilde, *The Importance of Being Earnest* (London: Prestwick House, 2005 [1895]), Act I, p. 18.

6 Comment made by Sir Paul Nurse during the Westminster Abbey Institute Fellows' Programme.

7 See Immanuel Kant, *Critique of Pure Reason* (Cambridge: Cambridge University Press, 1998 [1871]).

8 Cf. Rowan Williams, *The Edge of Words* (London: Bloomsbury, 2014).

9   Thomas Johnson (ed.), *Emily Dickinson*, *Complete Poems* (Boston, MA: Little, Brown and Company, 1960), no. 1129.

10   Georges Braque, *Illustrated Notebooks (1917–1955)*, trans. Stanley Appelbaum (New York: Dover Publications, 1971).

11   'An Anatomy of Truth: conversations on truth-telling with a politician, a journalist, a scientist and a poet', Westminster Abbey, 23 October 2013.

12   Matthew d'Ancona, *Post Truth* (London: Ebury, 2017).

13   Williams, *The Edge of Words*.

14   Said by a speaker at an Institute seminar under the Chatham House Rule.

15   Friedrich Nietzsche, *The Gay Science* (Cambridge: Cambridge University Press, 2001 [1882]), p. 344.

16   Ibid., p. 344.

17   Anthony Trollope, *The Way We Live Now* (London: Penguin Classics, 1994 [1875]).

18   Arthur Koestler, *Darkness at Noon* (London: Vintage Classics, 2019 [1940]).

19   George Orwell, *Nineteen Eighty-Four* (London: Folio Society, 2014 [1950]).

20   Vita Sackville-West, *All Passion Spent* (London: Virago Classics, 1987 [1931]), frontispiece.

21   Tom Stoppard, *Jumpers* (London: Faber and Faber, 2014 [1972]), Act I, p. 48.

22   Niccolò Machiavelli, *The Prince* (London: Penguin, 2011 [1532]) pp. 69–70.

23 Immanuel Kant, *The Doctrine of Virtue*, trans. M. J. Gregor (Philadelphia: University of Pennsylvania Press, 1971), p. 93.

24 Quoted in D'Ancona, *Post Truth*, pp. 9, 14.

25 Ibid., p. 28.

26 Orwell, *Nineteen Eighty-Four*, p. 229.

27 Quoted in D'Ancona, *Post Truth*, p. 52.

28 Sinan Aral, Deb Roy and Soroush Vosoughi, 'On Twitter, false news travels faster than true stories', research project for MIT, 8 March 2018, available at http://news.mit.edu/2018/study-twitter-false-news-travels-faster-true-stories-0308 (accessed 13 January 2020).

29 Simon Schama, *The Obliterators*, BBC Radio 4, broadcast on 28 February 2016, available at www.bbc.co.uk/programmes/b071s6nr (accessed 20 June 2020).

30 Committee on Standards in Public Life, *The Seven Principles of Public Life* (London: CSPL, 1995).

31 Janet Soskice, 'Truth and Beauty', lecture delivered in Westminster Abbey on 8 March 2018.

32 Richmal Crompton, *Still – William* (London: Macmillan, 1984 [1925]), pp. 153–73.

33 Shakespeare, *King Lear*, ed. R. A. Foakes, Act IV, Scene 6, ll. 170–72.

34 Ipsos MORI, 'Veracity Index 2019: trust in professions survey', Ipsos MORI Social Research Institute report, available at www.ipsos.com/sites/default/files/ct/news/documents/2019-11/trust-in-professions-veracity-index-2019-slides.pdf (accessed 7 January 2020).

35 Ipsos MORI and King's College, London, 'Political
    Leadership Poll 2014', available at www.ipsos.com/ipsos-
    mori/en-uk/kings-college-london-ipsos-mori-political-
    leadership-poll, Table 64 (accessed 13 January 2020).

36 Attributed to Harold Macmillan as an answer to the
    question of what blows a government off course. The
    Covid-19 pandemic has proved these words all too true.

37 Andrew Kakabadse, 'Is Government Fit for Purpose?:
    The Kakabadse Report', 2018, available at https://
    civilservant.org.uk/library/2018-Kakabadse_Report.pdf
    (accessed 13 January 2020).

38 Part of the Judges' Oath sworn by all newly appointed
    judges.

39 See Jonathan Evans, *Secret Service in an Age of Open
    Information* (London: Haus Publishing, 2020).

40 Aral, Roy and Vosoughi, 'On Twitter, false news travels
    faster than true stories' (accessed 13 January 2020).

41 Karl Popper, *The Logic of Scientific Discovery* (London:
    Routledge and Kegan Paul, 1959).

42 Charles Darwin, *The Autobiography of Charles Darwin
    1809–1882* (London: Collins, 1958 [1887]), p. 69.

43 Told by Sir Paul Nurse to the Westminster Abbey
    Institute Fellows' Programme.

44 'The Report of the Iraq Enquiry', a Report of a
    Committee of Privy Counsellors, available at www.gov.
    uk/government/publications/the-report-of-the-iraq-
    inquiry (accessed 13 January 2020).

45 For a full discussion of this approach, see my essay
    'Moral Analysis' in Claire Foster-Gilbert (ed.), *The*

Moral Heart of Public Service (London: Jessica Kingsley
Publishers, 2017), pp. 43–59.

46   Gerald Durrell, *The Talking Parcel* (London:
      Lippincott, Williams and Wilkins, 1975).

47   George Orwell, 'Politics and the English Language', in
      Inside the Whale and Other Essays (London: Penguin,
      1957 [1946]), pp. 143–57.

48   Harold Evans, *Essential English for Journalists, Editors
      and Writers* (London: Pimlico, 2000).

49   An English translation by Alastair Reid of Pablo
      Neruda's poem 'Keeping Quiet' is available here:
      www.poetry-chaikhana.com/Poets/N/NerudaPablo/
      KeepingQuiet/index.html (accessed 19 June 2020).

HAUS CURIOSITIES

PUBLISHED WITH WESTMINSTER ABBEY INSTITUTE

The Power of Politicians
by Tessa Jowell and Frances D'Souza

The Power of Civil Servants
by David Normington and Peter Hennessy

The Power of Judges
by David Neuberger and Peter Riddell

The Power of Journalists
by Nick Robinson, Gary Gibbon,
Barbara Speed and Charlie Beckett

The Responsibilities of Democracy
by John Major and Nick Clegg

Integrity in Public Life
by Vernon White, Claire Foster-Gilbert and Jane Sinclair

*Secret Service: National Security in
an Age of Open Information*
by Jonathan Evans and Claire Foster-Gilbert

HAUS CURIOSITIES

Inspired by the topical pamphlets of the interwar years, as well as by Einstein's advice to 'never lose a holy curiosity', the series presents short works of opinion and analysis by notable figures. Under the guidance of the series editor, Peter Hennessy, Haus Curiosities have been published since 2014.

Welcoming contributions from a diverse pool of authors, the series aims to reinstate the concise and incisive booklet as a powerful strand of politico-literary life, amplifying the voices of those who have something urgent to say about a topical theme.

'Nifty little essays – the thinking person's commuting read'
– *The Independent*

*Britain in a Perilous World: The Strategic
Defence and Security Review We Need*
by Jonathan Shaw

*The UK's In-Out Referendum: EU Foreign
and Defence Policy Reform*
by David Owen

Establishment and Meritocracy
by Peter Hennessy

Greed: From Gordon Gekko to David Hume
by Stewart Sutherland

*The Kingdom to Come: Thoughts on the Union
Before and After the Scottish Referendum*
by Peter Hennessy

Commons and Lords: A Short Anthropology of Parliament
by Emma Crewe

*The European Identity: Historical and
Cultural Realities We Cannot Deny*
by Stephen Green

*Breaking Point: The UK Referendum
on the EU and its Aftermath*
by Gary Gibbon

Brexit and the British: Who Are We Now?
by Stephen Green

These Islands: A Letter to Britain
by Ali M. Ansari

Lion and Lamb: A Portrait of British Moral Duality
by Mihir Bose

Drawing the Line: The Irish Border in British Politics
by Ivan Gibbons

Not for Patching: A Strategic Welfare Review
by Frank Field and Andrew Forsey

A Love Affair with Europe: The Case for a European Future
by Giles Radice